United Stat

MW01253218

EASY OLYMPIC SPORTS READERS

U S A

36 USC 380

SPEED SKATING
LONG TRACK

Griffin Publishing Group
Glendale, California

Speed skaters race.

Speed skaters race on
a track.

The speed skating track
is on ice.

The track is oval and has
two lanes.

Men race against each other.

Women race against each other.

Speed skaters wear skates with long, thin, flat blades.

They wear tight suits to help them go fast.

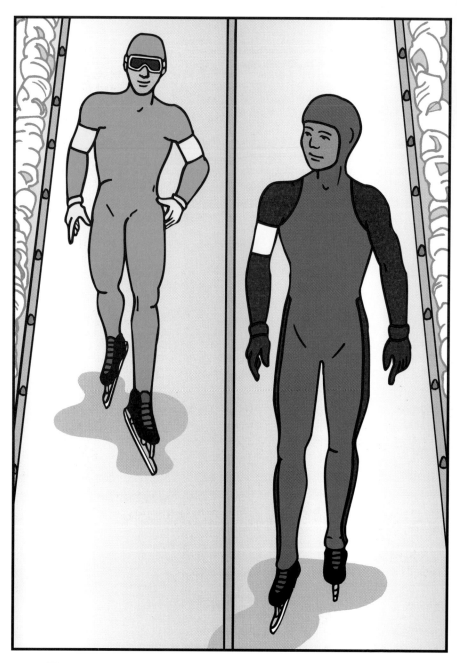

In each race, the skaters
race two at a time.

The pair begins at the
starting line.

Speed skaters push and glide on the straight parts of the track.

Their legs cross over
around the curves.

The skaters switch lanes
each time they go around
the track.

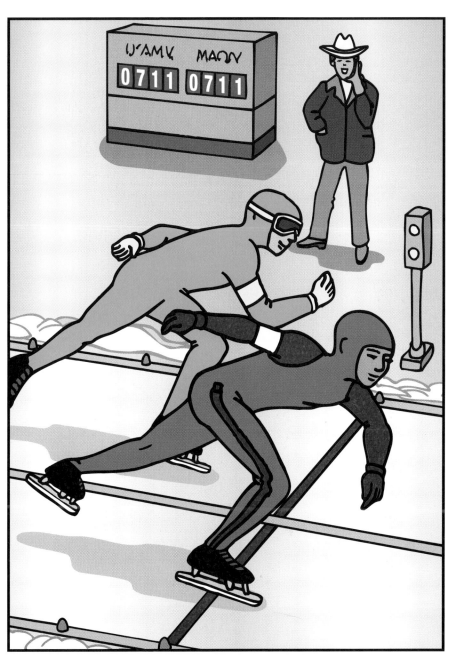

Each skater is timed by a
special clock.

After all pairs have finished, the skater with the fastest time wins.